Meditations on the Lord's Supper

Meditations on the Lord's Supper

by

John Willison

REFORMATION PRESS

Published by
Reformation Press, 11 Churchill Drive, Stornoway
Isle of Lewis, Scotland HS1 2NP

www.reformationpress.co.uk

FIRST REFORMATION PRESS EDITION – January 1990

SECOND REFORMATION PRESS EDITION (WITH REVISIONS)
November 2014

British Library Cataloguing in Publication Data

ISBN 978-1-872556-10-9

© Reformation Press 2014

FIRST KINDLE EDITION
ISBN 978-1-872556-11-6
© Reformation Press 2014

PRINTED BY
www.lulu.com

All rights reserved. No part of this publication may be reproduced, stored in a retrieval system, or transmitted, in any form or by any means, without the prior permission in writing of Reformation Press, or as expressly permitted by law, by licence, or under terms agreed with the appropriate reprographic rights organisation.

Contents

Foreword	7

Part 1 - Meditations before the Lord's Supper

Meditation 1	13
Meditation 2	16
Meditation 3	19
Meditation 4	22
Meditation 5	25
Meditation 6	28
Meditation 7	31
Meditation 8	34
Meditation 9	37

Part 2 - Meditations after the Lord's Supper

Meditation 10	43
Meditation 11	45
Meditation 12	47
Meditation 13	50
Meditation 14	52

Meditation 15   54
Meditation 16   57
Meditation 17   60

Part 3 - A personal covenant with God
Willison's personal covenant   65
Guidance for drawing up a personal covenant   71

Foreword

John Willison was one of the most outstanding evangelical ministers of the Church of Scotland in the eighteenth century. He was born near Stirling in 1680 and was brought to the saving knowledge of Christ at an early age. God called him to the ministry of the Gospel and in 1703, when he was aged 23, he was ordained as a minister in the Parish Church of Brechin, 27 miles (43 km) north of Dundee.

From the outset of his labours, Willison was distinguished by a zeal for the glory of God. He was a diligent pastor, and had a particular concern for the spiritual welfare of young people in his congregation. The excellent *Shorter Catechism* of the Westminster Assembly of Divines formed the basis of instructing them in divine Truth.

For men like Willison, the purpose of catechising was not simply to elicit memorised answers. He went beyond this, using further questions and answers to instruct the congregations in the doctrines which are so clearly taught in the *Westminster Confession of Faith* and the *Shorter Catechism*.

Willison excelled in catechising due to his skill in using clear and simple language. This attention to careful instruction of the young bore fruit under the blessing of God. As the years progressed he had the satisfaction of seeing the Lord's work prosper among his congregation in Brechin and subsequently in the South Church, Dundee, where was the minister from 1718 until his death in 1750.

Willison's labours were to become known to a wider audience. He soon gained renown for his catechetical and devotional writings. His *Mother's Catechism* is still in print (Free Presbyterian Publications) and it amply demonstrates his ability to instruct even the very young in simple language.

Much of Willison's published work is concerned with the sacraments, in particular the Lord's Supper. Valuable teaching is contained in his *Sacramental Catechism*. The character of Willison as a pious, heavenly-minded servant of God is seen very clearly in his sacramental sermons and meditations.

John Willison had that solemn view of the Lord's Supper which is rarely encountered in our day. Moreover, he knew the concerns and desires of God's people approaching the ordinance, and so he was able to speak words in season to them. These are reasons why the present work has always been so highly valued.

Some background information may be useful for readers unfamiliar with the Scottish Presbyterian mode of observing the Lord's Supper, known as Communion seasons. The practice of holding communion seasons, once universal throughout Scotland, has now largely disappeared, with some notable exceptions. At such seasons, Thursday is the "fast day", a day for confession of sin. Friday is the day of self-examination, and Saturday is the day of preparation for the solemn events of the communion Sabbath. Thanksgiving services are held on the Monday. The Lord often gave a great blessing during these five days of communion seasons, not only to communicants but also to the unconverted in bringing them to a knowledge of Christ.

The Lord's Supper was regarded in theological terms as *sacramentum nutritionis* – a sacrament of nurture – for the Lord's people. Only those with an accredited profession of faith in Christ were admitted to the Lord's Table, after examination by the Kirk Session, which consisted of the Minister and the ruling elders of the congregation.

Thus it may be seen that publicly professing faith in Christ and remembering the death of Christ at the Lord's Table were considered as steps not to be taken lightly. With this in view, the reader may see why Willison wrote the *Meditations*, particularly with young communicants in mind. The first nine meditations are concerned with the period before the Lord's Supper; the remaining eight, for afterwards.

John Willison's written works used to be common reading matter among spiritually minded people in Scotland and far beyond. Sadly, his collected *Works* were last issued in 1866 and second-hand copies are scarce. It is gratifying that individual works have been reprinted in recent years. His valuable writings deserve a much wider circulation.

Meditations on the Lord's Supper was the first publication issued by Reformation Press at its inception in 1990. It was greatly appreciated and rapidly went through two substantial print runs. Light editing has been undertaken for this new edition, largely to incorporate modern conventions of punctuation. Explanations of unfamiliar terms and Scots words are given in brackets. The publisher hopes that this further reprint and the e-book version will be profitable to many under the blessing of God.

The Publisher – Stornoway, November 2014

Part 1

Meditations before the Lord's Supper

Meditation 1

God's mercies to me have been very great and distinguishing. I was born in a valley of vision. I dwell in a lightsome Goshen, when many others are covered with Egyptian darkness and sit in the region of the shadow of death. I hear heaven's free market-day of grace proclaimed, when others are trysted with silent sabbaths. I am invited to a rich gospel feast, when others are trysted with a famine of the Word of God.

It is a great privilege that I am allowed to speak to God in prayer or hear from him in his Word. But how great is the honour he puts upon me when he invites me to a communion with himself at his holy table, where I may feast upon the fruits of Christ's purchase and hear him say to the guests, "Eat, O friends; drink, yea, drink abundantly, O beloved."

I am unworthy of the least crumb that falls from his table, far less of being admitted to sit with him at the table and eat of the children's bread. But since he is pleased to honour me so far as to call me to the marriage supper of the Lamb, O that he could also give me the wedding garment, prepare my unprepared heart and grant me all the sacramental graces, that I may be able to attend and entertain the King of glory!

O for spiritual hunger and thirst for the soul-feast, the heavenly manna and water of life that is to be set before me!

O that I had wells digged in this valley of Baca, that heaven's rain would descend and fill the pools, that so the wilderness might be turned into a fruitful field, and the dry land of my heart into springs of water, and my barren soul might blossom as the rose and send forth a smell as of a field which the Lord hath blessed!

I am now to ascend Mount Calvary and go to the place where Christ is to be set forth as crucified before my eyes. O that there I may look on him whom I have pierced, and mourn for sin that made the nails and drove them into my Redeemer! O that I may receive a broken Christ into a broken heart! O that the blood of Christ, which speaketh better things than the blood of Abel, may there plead with God for me, answer all the challenges of the law, and speak peace to my conscience! Let him there kiss me with the kisses of his lips and enable me to embrace him in the arms of my faith, saying, "This is my beloved, and this is my friend." O for a lively and strong faith, that I may take and hold a strong grip of my Redeemer, and that like the spouse I may say, "I held him, and would not let him go"!

Alas for my weak and slippery-fingered faith, that oft lets Christ go when I have fair occasions of getting grips of him! Oft do I lose my grips; Lord fasten them better. If Christ did not take faster grips of me than I do of him, my soul would have been in the devil's grips without relief. Ever blessed be his name for the strong grips he took and held of elect sinners on the cross! Yea, so sure and fast were they that that neither death nor devils, the wrath of God, nor curses of the law, could ever make him loose them again. Many waters could not quench his love, neither could the floods drown it. His love was stronger than death. O where is my love to him? O that the infinite love of Christ in dying on a cross might kindle in my frozen heart this sacred fire of love to him, that might burn up all my lusts and idols as stubble and make me cry out, "None but Christ, none but Christ!"

Meditation 2

I was entered into covenant with God by baptism, and was then brought under strong engagements to be the Lord's. But O! I have broken my covenant and backslidden from Christ. If I were under the law or a covenant of works, I would be utterly undone. But, blessed be God, I am under the tenders of a covenant of grace that admits of repentance and a surety for the guilty criminal, and graciously promises pardon to the penitent believer – nay, it promises repentance to the hard-hearted and faith to the unbelieving, and pressingly invites backsliding children to return to God through a Mediator.

I do here take hold of this gracious and well-ordered covenant; Lord, seal it to me at thy table. What shall I render to the Lord for instituting this ordinance, for leaving this precious legacy and token of love to his church, for preserving it to this age and continuing it in this land, and particularly for sparing and allowing me to come unto it? Glory to God that I see the seal of this covenant, that I see this welcome rainbow, appearing in the clouds of wrath as a sign and token of God confirming his covenant to believers and securing them against a destroying deluge.

Blessed be God that I am neither among Jews nor pagans upon earth, nor devils or damned souls in hell. I thank the Lord of heaven and earth that the things which were hid from the wise and prudent are now revealed unto babes, and that my eyes see and ears hear that which many prophets and kings desired to see and hear, and yet might not, and that now life and immortality are brought to light by the gospel.

O what would fallen angels and damned spirits give for such a day and such a prospect as I have? Lo, fire and brimstone from heaven are rained upon them, while manna is rained upon me. O that the solemn day I have in view may indeed be a day of the Son of man, a day of his power, and a day in his courts, better and sweeter to me than a thousand!

O that the holy table I am going to may be richly furnished by the great Master of the feast! O that he may grace it with his own presence and abundantly bless the provision, that by it the starving creature may be fed, the needy beggar may be satisfied, the hard heart may be softened, the cold affections warmed, the cloudy soul brightened, the straitened heart enlarged, the dim eye enlightened, the wandering mind fixed, and the doubting soul resolved! O that it may be a feast of fat things full of marrow, a meal signally blessed from heaven to me, that it may prove life to my soul, death to my sins, strength to my grace and poison to my lusts! Lord, let my heart begin to burn when I see the elements. Let my bands be loosed when I touch them. Let mine eyes be enlightened when I taste them. And let my whole soul be strengthened when I partake of them.

O that in receiving the bread and wine I may be enabled to receive Jesus Christ into my heart and may thereby get true and real infeftment [Scottish legal term: conveying legal right to ownership] of all Christ's purchase and a valid and unquestionable title to the everlasting inheritance sealed and confirmed to me!

Lord, make thyself known to me in the breaking of bread. Manifest thyself to me, as thou dost not do unto the world.

O bring me into the banqueting house and let thy banner over me be love! Lord, come to the feast, for it will be a dead and heartless feast if thou be absent. Sit thou at the head of the table, carve everyone their portion, and give me a Benjamin's mess (if it be thy will), that my soul may be satisfied as with marrow and fatness, and my mouth may praise thee with joyful lips. And when the King sits at his table, let my spikenard send forth the smell thereof. "Awake, O north wind; and come, thou south; blow upon my garden, that the spices thereof may flow out. Let my beloved come into his garden, and eat his pleasant fruits." O let my well-beloved come and feed among the lilies till the day break and the shadows flee away!

Meditation 3

Blessed are they that hear and know the joyful sound! But what will the news of Christ avail me without an interest in Christ? What will it profit me to have the Son revealed *to* me if he be not revealed *in* me?

O for the practical and experimental knowledge of Christ! Lord, hide not thyself from me. Stand not behind the wall, but show thyself to me through the lattice of ordinances. O draw by the veil of my guilt and make a display of thy glorious and attractive excellences, so that mine eyes may see the King in his beauty and my soul may be engaged to flee to him upon the wings of faith and love.

I am this day called to go to the table of this great King. But I am in a strait betwixt two. If I decline to come to this table, then I disobey my dying Saviour who commands me to show forth his death in this manner. If I come unworthily, then I fear lest I contract the guilt of his blood, and eat and drink my own damnation. Alas! My unworthiness makes me tremble to come. And yet my need pinches me so that I cannot stay away. Lord, to whom shall I go but to thee? For thou hast the words of eternal life.

Thou art my sun from whose beams I must receive the light of grace. Thou art the fountain from which I must draw living water. Thou art the root from which I must receive sap of increase. Thou art my head from whom I must get life and influence, so that without thee I am nothing, I have nothing, and I can do nothing. Let all my wants be upon thee and let all my supplies come from thee.

Surely, O Lord, the sea is not so full of water, nor the sun so full of light as thou art full of grace and mercy. O fill my narrow vessel out of thine inexhaustible fountain! Cast open the doors of thy treasures and let me have access to Christ's unsearchable riches. Are not these freely bestowed upon the needy without money and without price? O scatter thy bounty among poor beggars and let me be admitted to gather it! Let not such a miserable object go from thy door without an alms, for thou wilt not fail to give a crumb to me. O let not the needy be forgotten; let not the expectation of the poor perish for ever! Let none return ashamed from the fountain, who come expecting water.

Hast thou not said, "I will pour water upon him that is thirsty, and floods upon the dry ground"? And is there anyone more dry than I am? Or more poor and needy than I am? Lord, make me as thirsty as I am dry, as humble as I am poor, and as sensible as I am needy. Open my mouth wide, and then fill it. Alas! The voice of my prayer is weak, but O the cry of my wants is strong! Lord, hear that loud cry. Deal not with me according to my feeling and sense of need, which are small. But O deal with me according to my real necessity and thy royal bounty which is great beyond expression!

Lord, grace thine own ordinance and beautify the assembly of thy people with thy presence. Put the wedding garment upon the guests. Let thy spirit rest upon them. Let thy power be present to heal them, and cause thy glory to fill the temple.

O that God would bow the heavens and come down! O that he would touch the mountains (namely, my hard heart, unbelief, pride, worldliness, etc.), and cause them all to flow down at his presence! Let the Jordan of my lusts be driven back. Let the mountains skip like rams and the little hills like lambs. Let the earthly heart tremble at the presence of the God of Jacob. Let the rock be turned into standing water, and the flint into a fountain of water.

O come down as the rain upon the mown grass and as showers that water the earth, and revive all the withered roots of thy people! O for a shower from heaven, even a shower of the Holy Ghost, to make all their souls as a watered garden, that they might spring up as the grass, revive as the corn, grow as the lily, cast forth their roots, spread out their branches, and their beauty might be as the olive tree and their smell as Lebanon!

O if our Lord Jesus Christ's love and glory would come flowing like a full sea or the rushing of a mighty wind, and fill all the corners of his house and of his table, so that great grace might be on all his people! O to hear a sound of going in the tops of the mulberry trees, a sign that God is gone forth before us to smite the hosts of our lusts and to triumph over our enemies! O that the kindly breathings and prosperous gales of God's Spirit would enliven all the drooping hearts and fill all the empty sails of windbound communicants [i.e., like ships unable to sail because of a contrary wind]! O that the heavenly wind would blow from the right airt [quarter], that poor leaky vessels might come speed in their voyage and sail straight forward to the shores of Immanuel's land!

Meditation 4

How great is the divine goodness and condescension to me, in that he is pleased to allow me such near access to him! The men of Bethshemesh did not have liberty to look into the ark. But I have a warrant – yea, a command! – to contemplate a crucified Jesus, who is the image of the invisible God, the brightness of his Father's glory, and the express image of his person. Yea, not only to look to him, but also to touch him, handle his wounds, embrace his person and lodge him in my soul.

O Lord, I am not worthy that thou shouldest come under my roof; the house is so ruinous, smoky and defiled, thou hast not a fit place where to lay thy head with me. But, since thou didst not disdain to lie in a manger among beasts, nor to dine with Simon the leper, O come and furnish the house, prepare an upper room in my soul, and there abide and keep the passover with me! A look or word from thee would do it. Lord, speak the word, and thy servant's soul shall be healed and cleansed. Look upon me and be merciful unto me, as thou usest to do unto those that love thy name.

Happy would I be if I might get a heart-melting and soul-overcoming look of Christ's face at his own table, even of his face that is white and ruddy, and fairer than the sons of men. O for such a look as he gave to Israel when wallowing in his blood – a look that may cause me to live! O for such a look as he gave backsliding Peter – a look that may pierce my hard heart and cause me to weep bitterly! O for such a look as he gave Zaccheus – a look that might bring me speedily down from sins and idols, from my self-conceit and self-righteousness, and cause me to receive Christ joyfully into my heart!

Lord, give a look to all my idols that they may be discomfited, and give a look to my wandering heart that would bring it into a right frame for thy work. O come, put in thy hand by the hole of the door, and let heaven's sweet-smelling myrrh drop upon the handles of the lock, so that I may awake from my drowsiness and open all my doors to the King of glory! Come in, thou blessed of the Lord; wherefore standest thou without? Come and cast out all my idols – my worldliness, pride, prejudice, doubtings, and unbelief. Come and lay an arrest on all my wandering thoughts and call in my straying affections. Come and bind Satan, the enemy of my soul, and restrain him so as I may get my Saviour entertained and a match [betrothal] concluded between Christ and my soul at his own table. Come in, Lord, and abide in my heart as long as I abide here in the flesh. "Even so, come, Lord Jesus: come quickly."

O thou, who didst deliver Noah from drowning in the great deluge by the ark prepared for him, do thou deliver my soul from perishing in the fearful deluge of thy wrath by the ark Jesus Christ, whom thou hast prepared for saving heavy-laden sinners! O thou, who didst deliver Lot from Sodom and the flames of fire, deliver my soul from the Sodom of a natural state and from the flames of divine anger that will consume those that abide therein! O thou, who didst deliver Isaac from being slain and offered up a sacrifice by the lamb caught in the thicket, deliver me from being sacrificed to divine justice by Jesus Christ my propitiatory sacrifice, in whom thou art well pleased!

I am now to make a near approach to a crucified Christ, my ark and city of refuge. O to be safely launched therein! How sad will it be if I be found hovering outside the ark till the floods come and wash me off from the very side of it! And even when I see a window opened and mercy's hand put forth to take in poor, shelterless doves. How sad will it be eternally to be so near Christ, within a step of him, and never reach him, but perish like the thief upon the cross, with the Saviour at his side, and sink into hell between the outstretched arms of his mercy, and with his gracious calls sounding in my ears! What a woeful madness will it be to wilfully starve for hunger beside a rich feast that is prepared for the hungry – to perish for thirst near a full and running fountain – or to die in my wounds beside the balm of Gilead and the skilful physician there! Let me stir up myself in time to take hold of him.

When I approach so near a crucified Jesus in the Lord's Supper, O that I may with Thomas thrust my hand into his side, and also throw my heart into it! Let me not only behold the wounds of his side, his hands and his feet, but also by faith drink the water of life that runs from them and bathe my soul therein.

Meditation 5

The Lord is now calling me, as he did Moses, not out of the midst of a burning bush but out of the middle of the flames of his love. Put off thy shoes from thy feet, for the place whither thou goest is holy ground! O that I may put off the shoes of earthly affections, strip myself of worldly cares, and look narrowly to my steps when making such a near and solemn approach to the great Jehovah! Had not I been invited and commanded to come to his holy table, such a sinful wretch as I dared never have attempted it.

Instead of stretching forth a sceptre of mercy to invite me to his table, he might, with the rod of his wrath, justly have dashed me in pieces as a potter's vessel. Instead of entertaining me with the bread of life and the cup of blessing, he might have given me the bread and water of affliction – yea, he might have thrown me down there, where I should in vain cry out for ever for a drop of water to cool my tongue.

I am polluted and unfit to appear before God. But oh! They are undone, who keep away from him. I do not come to him because I am worthy but because he is rich in mercy and has contrived a way for saving such as I am. I come as the poor, starved wretch to the fire. I come as the hungry to be fed, as the naked to be clothed, as the sick and maimed to be recovered and healed, and as the unclean to be washed in the fountain opened to the house of David.

Lord, make this a healing ordinance to my diseased soul, and the savour of life to my dead heart. Make it also a sealing ordinance, to clear up to me the evidences of grace. Confirm to me the pardon of my sins and the assurance of thy love. O that I may so approach to Christ at his table, that I may return from it with my heavy laden soul disburdened and at rest, my conscience quieted, my corruptions subdued, my graces increased, my soul encouraged, my heart enlarged to run the way of his commandments!

Lord, increase my faith, excite my repentance, and warm my cold heart with affection to thyself. O that the love of God were shed abroad in my heart!

Lord, thaw my cold, icy heart with the beams of thy love and breathings of thy Spirit. May I have grace to wait closely upon God and attend all the motions of his Spirit. And when he draws, O cause me to run; when he knocks, O make me to open; when he blows, O help me to spread the sails; and when the waters are stirred, O let me put in for a cure! I am lying like the impotent man at the side of the pool. But of myself I am unable to step in and there is no man to put me into it. Nay, all the men on earth or angels in heaven cannot do it. Only the man Christ Jesus can give healing virtue to the waters of the sanctuary and apply them to me.

Lord, bless those who are to be employed as thy stewards at this solemn feast. Enlarge their hearts and open their mouths. Give them a door both of utterance and of entrance. Let them speak from the heart and to the heart. O make their tongues as refined silver, that their words may be powerful and pleasant, suitably and fitly spoken, like apples of gold in pictures of silver. And while they are busied in inviting, calling and serving others at thy table, let them not go unserved themselves.

O that thou wouldst descend at this occasion upon the mount, in sight of all the people! Let the Spirit of God, with his influences, be like Jordan at this season, to overflow all its banks. O for a blessed inundation and a high stream tide of that river, whose streams make glad the city of God! Lord, send a stream of it into every communicant's heart, and let mine be well watered and become like the garden of God.

O that I had Jacob's spiritual strength, I would wrestle with thee for thy presence and blessing to myself and others! I would even say, "I will not let thee go till thou bless me." Ah, Lord, I would have the blessing and keep thee too; for thy presence is the best of all blessings. And oh! It is a needful blessing at the solemn feast. What can thy people do there without thee? They will be no better than a company of dead carcasses set about thy table. There will be no life among them if the Lord of life be away. If thy presence, Lord, go not with me, carry me not up hence.

The desire of my soul is to thee and the remembrance of thy name, for there is none in heaven or earth but thou alone who can suit my soul's necessities. Nothing less than infinite mercy can forgive my sin. Nothing but infinite power can subdue my lusts. No less than infinite fullness can supply my wants. And nothing but infinite wisdom can guide me through this wilderness and bring me to Canaan above.

Meditation 6

Shall such a wretched dog as I presume to come unto thy table and eat of the children's bread? – I who am not worthy to gather the crumbs that falls from it. But I have heard of the mercy of the King of Israel, that he delights to show it to the unworthy, even to the chief of sinners. Lord, here is an object of thy pity. I am starving and have no bread, naked and have no clothing, wounded and have no cure, polluted and have no fountain, in debt and have no money, burdened and have no rest. Thus I have destroyed myself and have no remedy in myself. But in the name of the Lord Jesus I have a sure and all-sufficient help.

Lord, I have a multitude of sins and miseries, but thou hast a multitude of tender mercies. I have deep and heinous guilt, but thou hast a deep fountain to wash it out. Behold one depth calls to another – the depth of my misery to the depth of thy mercy. My sore is broad but thy plaster is answerable [correspondingly broad]. My wound is great but thy balm is excellent. O Lord, be merciful to me, heal my soul for I have sinned against thee!

Come, display the matchless excellences and healing virtue of thy balm at this time. And begin with my distempered soul and make experiment of it upon me. I am grievously stung with sin and Satan, these fiery serpents. But blessed be God for providing the brazen serpent and lifting it up on a pole, even Jesus Christ wounded and lifted up on the cross. O give me faith's eye to spy him thus lifted up under the symbols of bread and wine! O that I may lift up my eyes and see his healing wounds and feel healing virtue come from them to my wounded soul!

Lord, draw me, and I will run after thee. Cast a cord of thy love about my heart and hale me to thee. But O my heart, my soul, is heavy. I have great guilt and many lusts like lumps of lead hanging on me. How can I run and how shall I be drawn? But hast thou not said, Lord, "If I be lifted up from the earth, I will draw all men unto me" – sinners of all sorts and sizes? Surely a crucified Jesus lifted up on a cross, with his bleeding arms stretched out to embrace lost sinners, is the most attractive and drawing sight in the world. This wonderful lodestone [magnet] has drawn thousands of iron hearts to it at once, and shall my obstinate heart refuse to be drawn? O give me faith's eyes and let me see the glorious conqueror, Jesus, dying and drawing his poor captives home to himself, and let my heart be drawn with the rest!

Now the devil is holding and Christ is drawing. Now Michael and his angels and the dragon and his angels are striving about communicants' souls. O that Michael may prevail and his followers may be increased! O that the red dragon's head may be broken and may his interest get a fatal blow at this time!

Lovely Jesus, show thyself at this occasion through the lattice, for thou art fairer than the sons of men, more glorious than mountains of prey, and the chiefest among ten thousand. Thou art white and ruddy – white in regard of thy spotless innocence, and ruddy in regard of thy bloody passion [suffering]. And this matchless complexion makes thee altogether lovely in the eyes of all true believers. O bright morning star, I beseech thee to show me thy glory. Make thy holy table like mount Tabor to me, the mount of transfiguration, where I may get a heart-ravishing sight of Christ's beauty and such a view of his comeliness as may satisfy my mind, captivate my heart and make me long to be where I shall have the full and everlasting vision of his face.

Lord, meet with me at thine own table and show me a token for good. Deliver my soul from death, mine eyes from tears and my feet from falling. Rescue me from the fearful pit, bring me out of the miry clay. Set my feet upon a rock and establish my goings, and put a new song in my mouth, even praise onto our God. Behold, O God our shield, and look upon the face of thine anointed, even thy beloved Son in whom thou art well pleased. Lord, show thyself well pleased with me in him, and let me be accepted in the Beloved.

Lord, say unto my soul, "Fear not! I am thy salvation." Thy voice is sweet. O cause me to hear it! And make me hear thee so as I may follow thee, and follow thee so as I may find thee, and find thee so as I may never lose sight of thee again.

Meditation 7

O whither am I going? The place is holy, the table is holy, the bread I am to eat is holy, the cup I am to drink is holy, and God, who is infinitely holy, is terrible from his holy places. A wrong touch or look now is criminal and may cost me dear as it did Uzzah and the Bethshemites. This fearful breach that was made on them may cause me to tremble and cry out, "Who is able to stand before this holy Lord God?"

If John the Baptist (one of the greatest that was born of woman, and filled with the Holy Ghost from the womb) thought himself not worthy to unloose Christ's shoe, O how much more unworthy am I (the meanest of creatures; yea, a transgressor from the womb) to be admitted to touch, nay, feed upon Christ's broken body and shed blood!

If Peter, having seen Christ's glory and his own vileness, thought himself unworthy to be in the same ship with Christ, and cried out, "Depart from me, for I am a sinful man," how shall I, who am the chief of sinners, venture to sit at the same table with him and feed upon his flesh and blood?

If the poor woman, who had the bloody issue, feared to come and touch the hem of Christ's garment, how much more may I, who am full of the running issues of sin, fear to touch the sacred symbols of his body and blood, and to put my hand into his wounds and feel the print of the nails!

Lord, if the holy angels, these pure and unspotted seraphim who burn in zeal for thy service, must even cover their faces before thee, O how dare I appear in thy presence, whose zeal is so languishing, whose love is so cold, whose mind is so earthly and prayers so dull?

But what shall I then do? Shall I, with those who were bidden to the king's feast, refuse and make my excuse? O, I fear then the king would be angry, declare me unworthy to taste of his supper, and swear in his wrath that I should never enter into his rest.

I confess, Lord, I am fallen asleep with the foolish virgins; I find no oil in my lamp to go and meet the Bridegroom at his table. But blessed be thy name, the market of grace is not yet ended! I will therefore go presently to those that sell it, not to the merit of saints or blood of martyrs, but to Jesus Christ himself, who has graciously counselled me to buy of him tried gold and precious oil that will stand me in good stead in time of need. O that my oil and my lamp may be lighted at the beams of the Sun of righteousness, and so it shall never be put out!

Many pieces of furniture [provision] do I need – I want [lack] the girdle of sincerity, the shield of faith, the helmet of hope, the sword of the Spirit, the breastplate of righteousness, and to have my feet shod with the preparation of the Gospel of peace. But praises to my Redeemer and captain of salvation that hath provided a full storehouse and armoury to answer all my soul's necessities! O that out of his fullness I may receive grace for grace!

Lord, these things are so valuable; I have not wherewith to buy them, for I am wretched, miserable, poor, blind and naked. But good news! The poorest person in the world can make this purchase, for all Gospel-wares and commodities are bought without money and without price. O let me win to [reach] this cheap market and be content to take all out of Christ's hand as a free gift, disclaiming any worthiness in myself!

Lord, furnish me freely with all the qualifications of grace which I need. And when I come and offer my gift at thine altar, I'll say with David, "All things come of thee, and of thine own have I given thee." For what have I but what I have received? Nay, I'll join with the redeemed for ever in their song, "Not unto us, not unto us, but unto thy name be glory."

Meditation 8

If the centurion, whose faith was so strong and lively that Christ said he had not seen such faith in Israel, yet was fain to say to Christ, "Lord, I am not worthy that thou shouldest come under my roof," what shall I think of myself, who have so little faith and so much unbelief? Can I think myself worthy that Christ should come into my heart? O! I am utterly unworthy of such a guest. But seeing so great a King is willing to lodge in so poor a cottage, Lord, send beforehand and furnish it for thyself. O let thy spirit come and adorn the upper room and make me all glorious within! O for a penitent soul and believing heart!

Moses of old, with his rod smiting the rock, brought forth running water. O if Christ with the rod of his Word would but touch my heart, it would soon melt into tears of repentance! Alas! My heart will neither break nor melt till the Spirit of Christ come and deal with it. Lord, though I have not tears enough with Mary Magdalene to wash thy feet, yet thou hast blood enough to wash my feet, head, heart, hands and altogether. O bring my polluted, impenitent heart to the fountain. I know nothing will bring tears from mine eyes and sorrow from my heart if a believing view of that blood does not do it.

O for the eyes of faith to look to Golgotha and Gethsemane, and view Christ's agony and bloody sweat and the plentiful streams of his blood that flowed down from the cross! O that I could remember the wormwood and the gall, the cries and tears, the curses and pains, the desertion and anguish, which my sins brought upon the Son of God! O how did they pierce his head with thorns, his hands with nails, his side with a spear and his heart with sorrows! O the sharpness of that sword that pierced his soul! O the bitterness of that cup which he drank for me – a cup all mingled with the guilt of my sins and the curses of a broken law! Can I go to his table, look to his bleeding wounds, hearken to his dying groans, see my Redeemer's heart melted like wax, and yet my heart continue hard and unbroken? Shall the rocks rend sooner than my heart?

O my soul, where is thy faith? Where thy bowels? Where thy gratitude? Where thy humanity? Come then, behold the Author of life becoming obedient unto death, the spring of blessedness underlying the curse, the fountain of happiness thrown into misery – nay, into hell – and all to save me from it.

O behold thy glorious Surety with his head bowing on the cross and inclining to die! Behold his innocent hands, that healed all sorts of diseases and were still doing good, pierced and besprinkled with his own blood. Behold his feet, that never stood in the way of sinners but always walked in the law of the Lord, fastened to the cross with sharp and long nails. Behold his side, opened with a cruel spear, all red with his own blood. Behold his bowels that yearned for sinners, now shrunk and dried up.

Behold his face, that was fairer than the sons of men, now defiled with the spittings of the ungodly. Behold his mouth, which spake as never man spake, which hath no other refreshment but of vinegar and gall. Behold his ears, which were wont to hear the angels' praises, now ringing with the mocks and blasphemies of the wicked. Behold these eyes, which were brighter than the sun, now darkened with the shadow of death.

O! Now I see the Sun of righteousness under a fearful eclipse. I see his spotless soul covered with the black clouds of the Father's wrath. I see the heavens shut and darkened against him in the time of his distress. I see his royal visage turned pale, his strength dried up like a potsherd, his tongue cleaving to his jaws, and the streams of his precious blood watering his pierced feet.

O shall I thus see the innocent Lamb of God falling a sacrifice to incensed justice for my heinous guilt, and not loathe myself for all my abominations? O cursed sin, the murderer of the Son of God! Shall I ever harbour it any more? O let me never look upon it without tears of grief, nor think of it without indignation and rising of heart! O that henceforth the face of sin may be more frightful to me than hell, and temptations to sin more terrible than death!

Meditation 9

Under the law, they who had touched the dead were forbidden to come near the altar upon which were offered sacrifices that were but types of Christ upon the cross. And shall I, who am by nature dead in sins and trespasses and perform nothing but dead works, be allowed to approach that holy table where a living Saviour and a living God are present?

Blessed be the Lord Jesus that has come to visit the dead, though rotting and stinking in the grave. O that I may be raised up by the word of his power, as Lazarus of old was, and all my bonds loosed, that I may be at liberty to worship and serve him! And O that I may be allowed to be at the table with him, as was Lazarus after he was raised by him from the dead!

Lord, though I be dead in sins and trespasses, yet the bread which thou hast prepared cannot only strengthen the living but can also give life to the dead. Art thou not the resurrection and the life, who canst raise the dead to life and call things that are not as though they were? O cause me to hear thy quickening voice!

Blessed be God for the encouragement he has given me to come to this great feast – it being a feast of charity – to which are invited not the rich but the poor, maimed, lame and blind, who cannot make any return to the Author of it. My blessed

Saviour, while he was on earth, disdained not to eat with publicans and sinners. And surely though he be now highly exalted in glory, he still retains the bowels of a man, and all the pity and charity to perishing souls that ever he had.

Lord, I am polluted, but will not despair, for with thee is the fountain of salvation. I am poor, but will not despond, for thou art Lord of the whole earth, and openest thy treasures to the needy. I am naked, but I will not run away like Adam and hide myself from thee because I am so. But I will come with the more speed to thee to cover me with the wool and fleece of the Lamb of God, even the spotless righteousness and innocence of my Saviour. All my righteousnesses are as filthy rags; but, Lord, clothe me with the goodly raiment of my elder Brother which hath a sweet smell in thy nostrils, that therein I may obtain the blessing of my Father and a title to the inheritance. And let me by my Saviour's grace be enabled to offer thee a sincere and contrite heart, which is a savoury meat in which thou takest special delight. "A broken and a contrite heart, O God, thou wilt not despise." Lord, break my hard heart.

And will God, in very deed, dwell and converse with men – yea, sinful men? With thee, Lord, is great and terrible majesty. Nay, to the wicked and Christless thou art a consuming fire. But, glory to thy name, I see thee seated upon a throne of grace, that a poor sinner like me may draw near and converse with thee. Yea, I see a rainbow about thy throne, a sure token of thy mercy and willingness to be reconciled to sinners through thy Son Jesus Christ. I see the in the Word and sacraments, reaching forth thy sceptre of grace, that I may come and touch the top of it and live. Lord, all my hope is in the mercy of thy bowels and the merits of Christ's death. Surely thou art more ready to give than I am to ask, and more willing to forgive than I am to repent.

I am now going to a great feast. Lord, forbid it would be to me like Belshazzar's feast, he who in the time of it perceived a hand writing his condemnation. But O that I may see the finger of God writing my eternal absolution and assuring me that God will not enter into judgement with me! And, as of old thy gracious presence in Solomon's temple was manifested by the fire which came down from heaven and consumed the burnt offering, so I beseech thee to send from heaven into my heart the fire of thy love, to consume my lusts, kindle my affections to thee, and make my prayers more fervent.

Lord, thou usest not to send beggars away from thy house without an alms. Yea, thou hast oft been found of them that sought thee not, and hast made surprising and unexpected visits to poor souls and made them, before they were aware, like the chariots of Amminadib. O that I could win near hand Christ at his table! O that I may be allowed to kiss his feet, hear his voice, feel the smell of his garments and the savour of his sweet ointments!

Amen.

Part 2

*Meditations after
the Lord's Supper*

Meditation 10

What shall I render to the Lord for all his gifts and benefits unto me? The royal Psalmist admires divine goodness in causing the sun, moon and stars to shine in the firmament for man's behoof, and cries, "What is man that God is mindful of him?" But surely more cause have I to cry so, when I consider how God has caused the Sun of righteousness to shine on me in the firmament of Gospel ordinances and made that dayspring from on high to visit me. O that I may find this heavenly light shining into my heart!

The same Psalmist also exalts God's goodness in giving the beasts of the field, fowls of the air and fishes of the sea to be food for man. But far greater cause have I to praise God's infinite mercy for giving me the flesh and blood of his only Son to feed and preserve the life of my soul.

The poor woman of Canaan asked only leave to gather the crumbs which fell from the children's table. But unworthy I have been admitted to sit at the table of the Lord and eat of the children's bread. Nay, I have been invited to eat heartily and drink abundantly. Seeing then that I have eaten of Christ's meat, O that I may travel a good journey and work a good turn for Christ in the strength of it! O that I may be a diligent and faithful servant to so good a Master! Lord, I have eaten of thy bread; let me never lift up the heel against thee.

Nay, Lord, I have gone to thy table and adventured to seal a marriage contract with Jesus Christ as my Lord and Husband. I am indeed a black and uncomely bride, but my glorious Husband can beautify me with his perfect comeliness put upon me. Let me for ever discharge my old husbands and lovers – the law, my own righteousness, the world, my lusts and idols – and never have any hankering thoughts after them. O that I may be looking long and providing for the marriage day! The Bridegroom is ready long since. O that I were ready to go forth and meet him! That will be a glorious day when he shall rend the clouds, come down and set tryst with me in the air, and send his angels to carry me up to meet with him there. Why then does he delay his coming? Not because he is unready, but because I am not ready and all the elect are not yet gathered in. O that I were made meet and prepared for his coming, and that my heart and thoughts were still with him!

I have now a journey to go and a race to run, even a race to heaven, and I have great need of strength and direction in it. O if Christ would take me up into his chariot of salvation, that is all paved with love, how easily would I sit and how safely and pleasantly would I travel in the King's high road towards Immanuel's land! What sweet views and prospects would I get from Christ's triumphal chariot! O the lovely hills, the fruitful valleys, the pleasant rivers, the fair gardens and nourishing trees which I might see in the heavenly Canaan! What ivory palaces, golden streets and gates of pearl might I see in the new Jerusalem! If I could travel in Christ's company, my journey would not be tedious to me.

Meditation 11

If he that lacked the wedding garment at the king's table was cast into outer darkness, where shall be weeping and gnashing of teeth, what shall become of those who have come to Christ's table not only lacking the wedding garment but even clad with Satan's livery, wearing the rags of the old man and drawing the chains of iniquity about with them? Lord, if thou hadst dealt with me and my fellow-communicants according to our sins – nay, according to our religious services – thou hadst made the congregation an Aceldama, a field of blood. Alas! We have mingled our sacrifices with our sins; no wonder though thou hadst mingled them with our blood. But blessed be thy name who, instead of destroying us with the breath of thy mouth, art pleased to bring forth such words of comfort to us. "I will not execute the fierceness of my wrath because I am God and not man. I am the Lord, I change not; therefore ye sons of Jacob are not consumed."

Merciful God, thou forbiddest men to give that which is holy to dogs or to cast pearls before swine. And yet in thy boundless compassion thou givest thy Son, who is the Holy One of God and the most precious pearl in heaven, to such miserable sinners as I am, even to me who have so often promised to live holily and to leave my sins, and yet have ever returned to my vicious course as the dog to his vomit again, and the sow that was washed to her wallowing in the mire.

But seeing God has been yet again offering and speaking peace to me, let me never again return to folly.

Lord, save me from making peace again with these lusts which nailed Christ's hands and made his soul heavy unto death. May I now be helped to abandon all my old sins and never venture again upon that which killed my Saviour, dishonours his Father, grieves his Spirit and damns my own soul.

Lord Jesus, undertake for me, deliver me from my spiritual enemies, especially from myself, and from my false and treacherous heart which has so often beguiled me and yielded me a prey to sin, Satan and the world, and will now be ready to do it over again if it be not prevented by thy grace. I have great need to be always near thee, for without thee I can do nothing but sin, I can do nothing but contract defilement for thee to wash, make wounds for thee to heal and take on debt for thee to pay. O Lord, my soul is often like a leaky vessel which is heavy laden and ready to sink; the tempest of wrath blows hard and threatens to overset [overturn] me. O that I may get my vessel to run ashore near the Rock Christ, so that if it break or shipwreck anywhere, it may be about the clefts of this Rock where many a shipwrecked perishing soul hath found safety! Who ever perished at Christ's lee-shore? Who ever drowned in the sea of wrath, who sincerely aimed to grip to and fasten upon the clefts of this Rock?

Meditation 12

The manna in the wilderness was lodged in the tabernacle and kept within a pure golden pot. And shall I lodge Jesus Christ, the manna that came down from heaven, in a corrupt and unclean heart? Lord, cleanse my heart from sin and furnish it with grace, that it may be fit for thy residence. O that by tasting of the manna I may find my soul strengthened and lusts weakened! O that by touching the border of Christ's garment I may feel a secret virtue gone out of him to stop the running issue of my corruption and heal all my soul diseases!

Jonathan's eyes were enlightened after he had eaten a little honey dropping in a wood. But I have been eating honey dropping from the Rock of salvation, Jesus Christ. O that I may find the eyes of my understanding illuminated, that I may clearly perceive the vanity of the world and excellence of Christ, the deformity of sin and beauty of holiness, the emptiness of my own righteousness and the all-sufficiency of Christ's merits!

Men admire Abraham's happiness in that he lodged angels. But how far greater is my happiness in lodging him whom the angels adore, and in whose presence they all cover their faces with wings and cry, "Holy, holy, holy, Lord God Almighty" and so on! O that I had suitable room and entertainment for so glorious a guest! Lord, thou must both fit the room and bring the entertainment with thee.

O be not a stranger unto me or a wayfaring man that only turns aside to lodge for a night! But let Christ dwell in my heart by faith. O that he may say of my heart, "This is my rest for ever; here I will dwell, for it I have desired it"! Lord, say this also of thy Zion in our land and establish thy throne among us.

Lord, thou hast promised many special blessings to the utmost ends of the earth and to the isles afar off in the sea, among whom we in this land are. O hasten the accomplishment of thy promises to these remote parts of the earth, and make the spirit of error, superstition and formality wholly pass out of them, that thy name may be great among us and in every place incense may be offered to thee, and a pure offering!

Lord, send the news of Christ to the heathen nations who have long dwelt in the region of darkness. How sad it is that God, who made all the world, should have so little of its service and that the devil who ruined mankind should have the far greater part of the world to adore and serve him! Alas that he should have so much to justify that usurped title of his, "The god of this world"! Lord, destroy his kingdom and hasten the downfall of Babylon. When shall the forty and two months be expired? Let the hills melt and the mountains flow down at the presence of the Lord, and the seven hills among the rest. O why is his chariot so long a-coming? Why tarry the wheels of his chariot?

Lord, remember the poor, blinded Jews, the posterity of Abraham, thy friend. O, we are many a prayer behind with them; they oft minded the little sister when she had no breasts, and now the elder sister hath none. O what shall be done for her in her desolate case? O that the Redeemer would come to Zion and turn away ungodliness from Jacob! Lord, lift up thy feet to these perpetual desolations, and let the receiving of them be as life from the dead.

Lord, plead for thy persecuted people all the world over. Let their enemies know that their Redeemer is mighty and will hear the size of the oppressed. Let the earth disclose her blood and no more cover her slain.

Meditation 13

O that I could wonder at the glorious Son of God who descended from the highest heavens! He took not on him the nature of angels, but the nature of man, and hath crowned it with glory and immortality. Yea, he hath carried it above all heavens, above the seats of angels, beyond the cherubim and seraphim, and hath placed it on the right hand of his eternal Father. And he hath likewise promised to exalt believers (whom he hath united to himself as members of his body) unto the same honour and dignity. Lord, what is man that thou art mindful of him? And what am I, the worst of men, that I should be admitted to share in these glorious privileges which Christ hath purchased?

O that I could sing a song of praise to my well-beloved, a song of his eternal love and glorious undertaking, a song of his passing through the Red Sea and fighting the red dragon, a song of his bruising the serpent's head and unstinging the king of terrors, a song of his victorious resurrection, triumphant ascension and glorious return! Lord, cheer up and tune my heart to sing a song of Zion and rejoice in Christ as my portion. Let me speak of the glorious honour of his majesty and declare his wondrous works.

Lord, revive the spirits and enlarge the hearts of all thy people! Give them high and exalted thoughts of Christ, that their souls may glorify thy name. Open their lips, that their mouths may show forth thy praise. O, Shall the wicked go singing and rejoicing to hell, and thy people go always drooping and sorrowing to heaven? Is there any master like Christ and can give any wages like to his? Let me never by my carriage bring up a bad report (as the unfaithful spies) upon Christ's way, or the land that is afar off.

Thou hast recorded many encouraging words for thy people's comfort. Thou hast said that light is sown for the righteous, and gladness for the upright in heart. O for a shower from heaven to make that seed to spring! Blessed be thy name, God's seed will not rot beneath the clods. It will spring up sooner or later. Let me support myself with the Psalmist's cordial, "The Lord liveth; and blessed be my rock." Why should believers look like dead men while their Lord liveth and their Rock standeth? Their hopes may die, their comforts die, their frames die, their relations, their gifts and outward means may all die. But good news! The Lord will not die; their Rock will not fall. No wonder though the disciples drooped and looked as dead men when Christ was dead and lying in the grave. But blessed be God! He is risen; he liveth and will die no more! I have these good news from his own mouth, "I am he that liveth, and was dead; and behold I am alive for evermore, Amen; and have the keys of hell and of death." Is my Redeemer jailer of the prisons of hell and the grave? Good news! He will not lock in any of his friends or lovers; none but his enemies and haters shall be made prisoners there.

Many are the comforts thou givest, Lord, unto thy people. But let me not adore thy comforts more than thyself, or love the apples of life more than the tree of life. Let Christ himself have still the chief room in my soul.

Meditation 14

Who can utter the mighty acts of the Lord? Who can show forth all his praise? From all eternity thou didst mercifully see man's misery and didst contrive a remedy for it. Thou providedst a Surety for him before the debt was contracted, and a Saviour before he was lost. Thy wrath soon broke out against the angels that fell. Thou didst not wait for their repentance, but presently condemned them to everlasting chains of darkness. But long hast thou waited on me; yea, followed me with mercy even after I had many times undervalued and trampled upon the great gift and richest jewel of heaven, Jesus Christ.

Heavenly Father, though I have been a prodigal and a runaway from thy house, yet graciously own me again for thy child upon my return. I am a poor, destitute orphan that can do nothing for myself. But in thee the fatherless findeth mercy. I am a helpless and needy child, hanging at the breasts of ordinances. O let them not prove dry breasts to me, nor let me suck wind or poison from them, as many do to their destruction. But let me suck the sincere milk of the Word for my growth and enlargement in thy ways.

Lord, thou has directed thy people "in malice to be children, but in understanding to be men". Many, alas, are found the very reverse of this: in understanding they are children, but in malice they are men. Lord, free me from the leaven of malice, pride and envy. Alas! I am a child in knowledge. O that I were such in duty and affection. Lord, make me like a little child, meek and humble, obedient and tractable, affectionate and full of regard to thee, my heavenly Father. O that I were born again and had the Spirit of adoption in me, enabling me to cry "Abba, Father", and inclining me to be much about my Father's hand. My needs are very great; but blessed by thy name thou has erected a throne of grace for me to come to in the time of need.

Many are the needs which thou hast left upon me, that I might have the more errands to thy throne and that thou mayest the more often hear my voice. Lord, pour out upon me a spirit of grace and supplication, and cause me to delight in approaching thee.

Lord, help me to remember the vows and solemn engagements I have been taking on. I have been giving thee my bond at a communion table for thankfulness, love and obedience. O let me have Christ's return-bond for my relief, that he will strengthen me by his powerful grace to pay my vows to God, for I do entirely distrust my own strength. O that my obedience may be universal, cheerful, constant, and growing like the morning light.

Give me grace always to believe and remember the end of my creation and the vanity of this world, the shortness of my life and the uncertainty of the time of my death, the miseries of such as die in their sins and the unspeakable joys of those who die in the Lord.

Meditation 15

I have been swearing allegiance to the King of heaven over the broken body and shed blood of his dear Son. And seeing I have now opened my mouth unto the Lord, O save me from going back! Yea, I have been enlisting myself as a soldier to fight under the banner of Jesus Christ as the Captain of my salvation. And my Captain has been giving me a feast to hearten and encourage me against all difficulties. O that I may be strengthened by it, to fight manfully against all his and my enemies; yea, and to prevail over them and to put to flight the armies of the aliens!

Alas! I must confess to my shame that I have often fainted and turned back in the day of battle. I have gone from Christ's standard into the enemy's camp. O for the shield of faith! O for grace to depend more upon my Captain for strength and furniture [provision], whether for work or warfare, duty or difficulty! Lord, leave me not to tug at the oar of unassisted endeavours, or to struggle with duty in my own strength, but help me always to look to my covenanted Lord for covenanted strength. O let covenanted grace be sufficient for me!

May I now be going on from strength to strength, from one degree of grace to another, from one evidence, experience and manifestation to another, till at length I appear before God in Zion. Let me forget those things which are behind, and reach forth unto those things which are before, and so press on toward the mark, for the prize of the high calling of God in Christ Jesus. And let me count all things but dung and loss, that I may win Christ and be found in him, not having my own righteousness, but his to clothe me.

My days are flying away as a swift post [despatch]; eternity is hastening on with winds. Much of my handbreadth of days is worn away and soon will my sun be turned and be very low. O that I may be near my lodging against [in preparation for] night! The blast of the last trumpet is at hand, and a proclamation will shortly be made by one standing in the clouds, that time shall be no more. O that I may improve precious time well while it lasts, and that I may run fast, with my eyes towards heaven as my home and everlasting lodging place!

It is an encouragement to run that Christ is in heaven before me; God send us a joyful meeting! Lord, give me the traveller's charges [provisions] by the way, something to sweeten my journey and make it lightsome. O where are the grapes of Eschol, the cordials of faith, the views of Canaan from Pisgah hill? O that I were frequently sending faith and hope, these two faithful spies, to survey the promised land, or at least to visit the borders and outer coasts of my Lord's country; that they might bring me back some encouraging reports to support and cheer my heart whilst in the wilderness.

Lord, my wants are many and I need daily supplies from thee. But blessed be God that I have such an Agent in heaven as Christ to present my bills, petitions and supplications! I put all my requests in his hand and leave them to his care and management, for he knows the fit time to present them and send me an answer of them. I desire to give him all my secret wishes and trust him with all my concerns.

Lord, stay not away from me, but let me have some gracious visits now and then in thine ordinances. Give me thy Holy Spirit to teach me when I am ignorant, to quicken me when I am dull, to awaken me when I am secure, to revive me when I am faint. Let thy good Spirit be still suggesting things to me and bringing thy Word and promises to my remembrance, that my hard heart may now and then gush forth in streams of love and desire towards thee. O divine Shepherd, thou hast refreshment for my weariness, guidance for my wanderings and balm for my wounds. O lead me into the pleasant pastures that are watered by the fruitful streams of thy Spirit, that so this tempest-beaten soul may at last be brought into the harbour of rest and be laid up securely with thee!

Meditation 16

Glory to God, that hath not withheld his Son, even his only Son, from me, but hath given him to be a propitiation for my sins – yea, and to be the life and food of my soul. Blessed be his name that he who offered himself for me upon the cross doth also offer himself to me at his table. O that the sacrifice of Jesus Christ, which he offered on the cross and which I have been commemorating at his table, may atone for all the failings and miscarriages both in my preparations and performances! O blessed for ever be the Lord Jesus for the wounds which he received on the cross for my sins! O print them deeply on my heart, that I may still remember them and continually bear about with me "the dying of the Lord Jesus", that the life also of Jesus may be manifested in me!

I have been eating the bread of my Father's house. O let me not return to feed on the husks of the world and sin! But as I have the Lord Jesus, so help me to walk in him. Uphold me by thy right hand and let none pluck me out of it. And according to the well-ordered covenant, put thy fear in my heart, that I may never depart from thee.

O thou that givest power to the faint and increasest strength to them that have no might, and who alone art able to keep me from falling, do thou stablish, strengthen and settle me. Lord, never leave nor abandon me to myself, otherwise I will be as a reed shaken with the wind and a leaf driven to and fro. Alas! My heart is like Reuben, unstable as water. O if it were liquid as water, that I might, like Hannah, pour it out in prayer before the Lord!

Lord, preserve any degree of softness of heart or liveliness of frame which thou hast wrought in me by thine own ordinance, and help me to improve it, otherwise the devil and the world will soon come and lull me asleep, and they will take away the living child and leave a dead one in its room. Screen me from the cold, chilling blasts that come from the devil and the world, that my love be not frozen up. But let the south winds of the Spirit come and kindly breathe upon any spark of grace which thou hast kindled, cherish convictions, preserve good motions and encourage desires.

O maintain the fire of thy love in me by the oil of thy gracious influences! Let the name of Jesus be always to me as precious ointment poured forth, that I may remember his love more than wine. And let the remembrance of his love be still efficacious to melt my hard heart, enliven my dead soul and inflame my cold breast with a burning affection to him. O let the charms of my Redeemer's love triumph over all the charms of sin's pleasures and Satan's devices, and cause me to reject all their solicitations with disdain and abhorrence! I have seen Christ's love in bleeding to death on the accursed tree to deliver me from lying in hell; let me never again wilfully walk in the road that leads to it. I have seen him wrestling in an agony to open heaven's gates for me; let me never turn my back on heaven and tell him by my unworthy carriage that he might have saved his labours. O let me never requite the kindness of my glorious friend at this rate!

O that I could spend my life admiring Christ's love and contemplating his beauty! Surely he is the Rose of Sharon – yea, the most beautiful Rose in all the garden of God, and that Rose that beautifies all the flowers in the garden. How charming is his beauty! And how fragrant is his smell! One leaf of this fragrant Rose is sufficient to perfume the whole creation. O let the Rose come and perfume my ill-smelling heart and ill-savoured performances, that God may not reject both me and them! Let the sweet savour of Christ's sacrifices and the odour of his intercession so diffuse itself and fill heaven, that the evil savour of my sins and duties may not enter. Surely if it were not for that sweet perfume, God would not suffer such a stinking dunghill as I am to approach so near him and be as a smoke in his nostrils all the day. O, if the wind of the Spirit would but blow the sweet smell of Sharon's Rose on my unsavoury affections and withered soul, it would soon revive and blossom as the rose, and the scent thereof would be as the wine of Lebanon!

Meditation 17

Christ is the glorious Bridegroom, whose beauty is surpassing, his kingdom mighty and his riches infinite. How marvellous it is that such a one should offer to match with [betroth] uncomely souls and court a bride naturally black as hell, and seek her through a sea of blood, through the pains of death, the torments of hell and horrors of the grave! How marvellous that he should follow me with his alluring invitations and Gospel offers in my wanderings through the wilderness of sin; yea, and present me with the rings and bracelets of his precious promises and Spirit's consolations, and all to win my heart and gain my consent to him!

He is my Lord and my God. Can my heart be but ravished with his love? He took shame and gave me glory; he took the curse and gave me the blessing; he took death and gave me life; he took my sins and gave me his righteousness. O wonderful and happy exchange for my soul that was ready to perish! My soul's blessing be evermore upon the head of him that made this exchange with me! O that I may be more and more acquainted with him and the way of salvation through righteousness and strength!

Let me still desire to go out of myself, that I may be found in him, not having my own righteousness but that which is through the faith of him. Let me always sit under the shadow of this Tree of Life which yields the richest fruits, and let those fruits be sweet to my taste. Blessed Jesus, thou art my life, my strength, my wisdom, my riches, my light, my health, my joy, my glory and my all in all. Be never far from me; but give me faith always to live in thee and depend on thee.

Lord, pity those poor souls who have been watching for the Son of David as he passed by in the ordinances, and yet are complaining that their eyes have not seen the King in his beauty. Draw aside the veil and show thyself to them. Lord, when thou showest thyself, let me love thee. And when thou withdrawest thyself, let me follow thee and lament after thee.

Lord, multiply the children of Zion, the sons born in thy house, even those who are begotten again to a lively hope. And when the Lord shall count and write up the people, may it be written of many in this land, that this man and that woman were born there.

Alas for the unsuccessfulness of sermons and sacraments in this age! Where is the power and life that used to accompany solemn ordinances? Where are those breathings, pantings, mournings, meltings, longings and heavenly frames of heart that were wont to be seen at such occasions? There was a day when one sermon pricked some thousands to the heart. But now many sermons are preached and sacraments dispensed, and scarcely any pricked to the heart for sin.

Lord, hasten the downfall of antichrist; remove that mother and mistress of abominations in the earth. Take graven images and superstition out of the way, and bring in the Jews in troops. Let the time come when this church shall sing for joy, when Scotland's moon shall shine like the light of the sun, and her sun like the light of seven days in one. Come and lay her stones with fair colours and her foundations with sapphires! Make her windows of agates and her gates carbuncles! Let the name of her cities be "Jehovah

Shammah" – the Lord is there. And let the inscription of the people's lives be "Holiness to the Lord". O that the pleasant flowers may appear and the time of the singing of birds may come!

Amen.

Part 3

A personal covenant with God

Personal Covenants

Preparation for the Lord's Supper was undertaken in a serious manner, with the glory of God and the spiritual advancement of the communicants in view. Willison wrote in an age when some communicants solemnly made personal covenants with God. He provides an example of this, with advice to those who wished to draw up their own covenant.

Willison's personal covenant

Almighty God and Creator of all things, thou didst make man at first upright and happy; but by the Fall he is become most sinful and miserable. I acknowledge that by nature I am an enemy to thee, a child of wrath, and a slave of sin and Satan. I have been a transgressor of thy laws from the womb and it is a wonder of thy patience that thou hast not made me a monument of thy wrath in hell long before this time. What will become of me to all eternity if I abide in this state?

I have heard that there is mercy in God to lost sinners through the blood of the crucified Jesus, which revives my drooping soul. Can this mercy reach the like of me? But surely the viler a sinner I am, thou hast the fairer opportunity of showing the freeness of thy love and the efficacy of thy Son's blood. And if I be a sharer of it, eternal hallelujahs will be sung to the Lamb of God on my account. I do therefore come and cast myself down at the feet of infinite mercy, and plead for it according to thy promise through Jesus Christ, thy dear Son.

O Father of mercies and Father of my Lord Jesus Christ, I am now sensible [cognizant] of my sin and folly in rebelling against thee and going over to Satan's camp. I desire to return as a penitent prodigal son to my heavenly Father, confessing my guilt, and willing to join myself unto the Lord in an everlasting covenant, never to be forgotten.

O Father, I have sinned against heaven and in thy sight, and am no more worthy to be called thy child. But I would think myself happy if I were admitted to the meanest station [position] or room in thy family. I desire to magnify thy free love and infinite wisdom in contriving a way of salvation to lost sinners through a mediator, and in sending thine eternally beloved Son to be the Mediator and Surety for satisfying thy justice for them, and for purchasing grace and glory to them.

According to thy command, I desire to put honour upon thy Son, and heartily to approve of this device of salvation, as every way worthy of God, and to fall in with it in all respects. O pity thine own creature, the workmanship of thy hands. Go over thy work again, and upon Christ's account create me anew after thine own image, that I may be fitted for thy service and glory.

O blessed Jesus, I admire thy love in undertaking to be the surety and sacrifice for lost sinners, and in making offer of thy blood to wash the like of me; welcome, Lord Jesus! I do hereby disclaim all other ways of salvation and betake myself to thee as my only Mediator and Saviour. I do embrace thee in all thine offices and give up myself to be saved, taught and ruled by thee.

I accept thee as my great High Priest, to atone for my soul and plead my cause with the Father by thy meritorious death and powerful intercession. I renounce all my own righteousness and worthiness in the business of justification and acceptance with God, and avouch thee alone as the Lord my righteousness.

I accept thee as my great Prophet, and give myself up to thy teaching and instruction, so that I may be conducted by thee through the wilderness and brought safe to heaven at last. O for wisdom to follow thy directions.

I accept thee as my King, swear allegiance to thee, and heartily consent to thy laws and government. Let thy throne be set up in my soul and let all thine enemies there be made thy footstool.

I accept thee for my Husband, and consent to the marriage covenant in all its articles. I accept thee as my Captain, and enlist myself as a soldier under thy banner to fight in thy strength against all thine enemies. I go in with all thy gospel terms, and am well pleased with the self-denying way of salvation proposed in them. I am content to be an eternal debtor to free grace and that the glory of my salvation be for ever ascribed to Jesus Christ my Surety.

O Holy Spirit, I thankfully accept thee as the applier of my Redeemer's purchase, and do welcome thee to do thine office in my soul, to work faith in me to believe the Gospel, to bring about the change of the new birth, and to renew all my faculties. To thee I am beholden for all the good motions and inclinations excited in me. O let them be continued and the good work carried forward in me to perfection. I do choose thee for my Quickener, my Sanctifier and my Director through all my pilgrimage. I yield myself to thine influences and conduct, and desire carefully to attend all thy motions and convictions, both in performing my duty and in abstaining from sin. O work grace in me for that effect, and enable me always to study and choose the things which are pleasing to thee.

According to my baptismal vows I do here renounce and abandon all the enemies of the Holy Trinity – the devil, the world and the flesh. And I do here surrender myself unto thee, Father, Son and Spirit, one God, to be thine and only thine, thine and not the devil's, thine and not the world's, thine and not my lusts', thine and not my own. I desire with my whole heart to choose and avouch thee to be my God and everlasting portion, and also to devote and dedicate myself, soul and body and all that belongs unto me, to be instruments of thy glory, and to be disposed of for thy use and service. O do thou henceforth set thy mark upon me, as a child born to thee and formed for thy praise. Stamp me with thine image, that I may be distinguished, set apart and consecrated for thy service and glory all my days.

And seeing above all that thou requirest the heart, I do here make an offer and surrender of my heart unto thee. Lord, take it and form it for thyself. Make it entirely new; make it soft, tender, pliable and holy. Put thy fear in it and write thy laws on it, that I may serve thee continually and never depart from thee. Lord, I here give my consent to thine entering in and taking possession of the throne in my soul. Be therefore cast open, all the doors of my soul, that the King of glory may enter in and dwell for ever. I have found my heart very corrupt, wicked and deceitful, and will no longer pretend to manage it; but I give it up to thee, to bring every thought and inclination into subjection to thee.

I see the world is nothing but vanity and vexation of spirit. I will never any more set my heart upon it, but rather endeavour to conquer it and subdue my inclinations to it. I place my happiness only in the enjoyment of God. I view heaven as my country and dwelling-place, and I will henceforth set my face heavenward, and spend my life here in God's service and in communion with him, that I may be meet for the heavenly state.

I will always look upon sin as the enemy of God and the crucifier of Jesus Christ my Saviour, and will pursue it to death. I will never follow a multitude to do evil, but will rather join myself to the people of God, though they be despised or persecuted. I take Christ with his cross as well as with his crown, and I cheerfully submit to the rod and discipline of his house.

Lord, if thou wilt undertake that thy grace shall be sufficient for me, I shall think nothing too difficult to attempt or too much to suffer for thee. I desire to learn the life of faith and of prayer. O teach me it, that I may make daily use of Christ my Surety, both for justification and sanctification, and for strength to perform duty, bear the cross and resist temptation. I look unto thee to send forth the Spirit into my soul, to assist and strengthen me for every good word and work.

Heavenly Father, I take thee for my Father, I take Christ for my life, I take the Spirit for my guide. I take thy Word for my rule, thy promises for my encouragement, thy testimonies for my counsellors, thy Sabbath for my delight, thine ordinances for my trysting-place, thy people for my companions, thy glory for mine end, holiness for my way, and heaven for my home.

Lord, I have no might or strength to keep or perform any thing I have engaged, but undertake all in my Surety's strength, depending upon his promise that he will never leave nor forsake me. In the Lord Jesus only have I righteousness and strength. O Lord, be Surety for thy servant for good, give always what thou requirest, then demand what thou pleasest.

And as an evidence of my sincerity in this solemn profession, dedication and engagement, I am willing to subscribe with my hand unto the Lord, as I am warranted, "Now I am thine; Lord save me."

Guidance for drawing up a personal covenant

As for those who may incline for a different form, and one that may be more suitable to their case, let them, for their help in drawing it up, bear in mind these four branches of a covenant transaction with God – renunciation, acceptation, dedication, engagements – and they may enlarge and be particular upon them, or any one of them, as this may best suit the conditions of their souls.

Under the head of renunciation, we may enlarge upon our abandoning and forsaking the world and its allurements of profit, pleasure, honour and power, Satan and all his tempting baits, the flesh and all its lusts, our beloved idols, our inward and outward sins, and our own righteousness in point of justification, and so on.

Under the head of acceptation, we may insist upon our choosing and closing with God the Father, the Son and Holy Ghost; Christ as a prophet, a priest, a king, a husband, a surety, a shepherd, a captain, etc.; God's covenant, his promises, his Word, his precepts, his sabbaths, his ordinances, his people, his providences, his rod, his cross, and so on.

Under the head of dedication, we may expatiate upon our resigning and giving up to God our souls, with all their faculties (understanding, will, memory, conscience) and their affections (love, hatred, joy, sorrow, hope, fear), our bodies with all their senses and members (heads, tongues, eyes, ears, hands, feet), our enjoyments and all the good things we possess (such as our health, strength, gifts, interest, wisdom, power, reputation, substance, relations, times, opportunities, and so on).

Under the head of engagement, we may run out in resolving, promising and vowing, in Christ's strength, to cease to do evil and learn to do well, to avoid all outward sins and those which have most easily beset us, whether lying, swearing, intemperance, unjust dealing, sabbath-breaking, and so on; to subdue all inward lusts, such as pride, passion, covetousness, unbelief, and so on; to perform all commanded duties, both inward and outward, such as keeping of the heart, believing, repenting, meditating, examining ourselves, reading, hearing, praying, family worship, sabbath sanctification, and so on; and also we must mind [remember] to engage to the life of faith, the life of prayer and thankfulness, the life of communion with God, the life of new obedience, and so on.

John Willison

www.ingramcontent.com/pod-product-compliance
Lightning Source LLC
Chambersburg PA
CBHW071413040426
42444CB00009B/2221